AND OTHER PSYCHOACTIVE CACTI

T0165587

"The white man goes into his church house and talks about Jesus; the Indian goes into his tepee and talks to Jesus."

Quanah Parker (1839-1911)

AND OTHER PSYCHOACTIVE CACTI

Adam Gottlieb

RONIN PUBLISHING, INC.
www.roninpub.com

PEYOTE AND OTHER PSYCHOACTIVE CACTI

ISBN: 0-914171-95-X
ISBN: 978-0-914171-95-9

Copyright 1977 by Kistone Press
Copyright 1997 by Twentieth Century Alchemist

Published by
RONIN PUBLISHING, INC.
PO Box 22900
Oakland, CA 94609
www.roninpub.com

Pages 44-66 "Cultivation of Peyote and Other Cacti" and photos copyright 1977 by Derek K. Westlund, reprinted by permission of author.

Project Editor: Sebastian Orfali
Editors: Adam Gottlieb, Leonard Mercado, and Derek Westlund
Cover Design: Judy July
Front Cover Photo: Adam Gottlieb
Back Cover Photo: Derek K. Westlund
Prepress: Generic Typography

ALL RIGHTS RESERVED. No part of this book may be reproduced or transmitted in any form or by any means electronic or mechanical, including photocopying, recording, or by any information storage and retrieval system, without written permission from the author or the publisher except for the inclusion of brief quotations in a review.

First printing 1997

Printed in the United States of America
Distributed to the book trade by Perseus/PGW

Notice to Reader

This book is a reference work made available for informational, entertainment, educational, archival and any other purposes protected by the First Amendment of the Constitution of the USA. The material in this book is for persons needing information, such as lawyers, law enforcement officials, substance abuse counselors, novelists, archivists, scientists and reseachers. It is not meant for minors and parents should exercise appropriate control. The author and publisher do not advocate breaking the law and make no express or implied warranties whatsoever, including but not limited to warranties of accuracy or reliability with respect to the information contained in this book. The author and publisher will not accept liability for any injuries or damages that may result from acting upon or using the contents of this book. Readers should consult appropriate legal, medical, scientific or spiritual experts before using any information in this book.

CAUTION: Extraction and other procedures involving volatile solvents are hazardous, potentialy explosive or toxic, and should be performed only in licensed labs by professional chemists. Some cactii and contaminants are poisonous and may have potential for causing illness and death. Extreme caution is required when identifying cactii, including corroboration by a botanist trained in species identification.

Picture Credits

front cover: photo by Adam Gottlieb
p. i, iii: illustration from *Eine Giftige Kaktee* (Paul Hennings)
p. vi: photo from Print Mint
p. viii: photo by Adam Gottlieb
p. 2: photos by Adam Gottlieb
p. 2: illustrations from *Design Motifs of Ancient Mexico* (Enciso, 1953)
p. 7: illustration from *Haight Ashbury Flashbacks* (Gaskin, 1990)
p. 10: illustration from *Le Peyotl* (Rouhier, 1927)
p. 12: photos by Adam Gottlieb
p. 15: photo by Adam Gottlieb
p. 16: illustration from *Memoirs of the American Museum of Natural History* (Lumholtz, 1900)
p. 18: illustration from *Design Motifs of Ancient Mexico* (Enciso, 1953)
p. 21: illustration from *Le Peyotl* (Rouhier, 1927)
p. 22: Reprinted from Barbara G. Meyerhoff: *Peyote Hunt: The Sacred Journey of the Huichol Indians* © 1974 by Cornell University. Used by permission of the publisher, Cornell University Press.
p. 24: illustration from *Design Motifs of Ancient Mexico* (Enciso, 1953)
p. 26: photo by Adam Gottlieb
p. 28: photos by Adam Gottlieb
p. 30: photos by Adam Gottlieb
p. 32: photos by Adam Gottlieb
p. 34: photos by Adam Gottlieb
p. 36: photos by Adam Gottlieb
p. 37: illustration from *Design Motifs of Ancient Mexico* (Enciso, 1953)
p. 38: photo by Adam Gottlieb
p. 40: photos by Adam Gottlieb
p. 42: photo by Adam Gottlieb
p. 44: photo by Derek K. Westlund
p. 45: illustration from *Le Peyotl* (Rouhier, 1927)
p. 46: photo by Derek K. Westlund
p. 58: photo by Derek K. Westlund
p. 70: illustrations by Adam Gottlieb
p. 74: illustrations by Adam Gottlieb
p. 76: photo by Jeremy Bigwood
p. 82: illustration from *Haight Ashbury Flashbacks* (Gaskin, 1990)
back cover: photo by Derek K. Westlund

Text Credits

p. vi: from *The Peyote Religion* (Slotkin, 1956)
p. 11: as quoted in *Peyote: The Divine Cactus* (Anderson, 1996)
p. 16: as quoted in *Plants of the Gods* (Schultes & Hofmann, 1992)
p. 18: from *The Doors of Perception* (Huxley, 1954)
p. 25: from *Plants of the Gods* (Schultes & Hofmann, 1992)
p. 26: from *Plants of the Gods* (Schultes & Hofmann, 1992)
p. 37: as quoted in *The Botany and Chemistry of Hallucinogens* (Schultes & Hofmann, 1980)

TABLE OF CONTENTS

San Pedro and Doñana

ＩNTRODUCTION

 Many people are already aware of the psycho-active effects of peyote. There are, however, numerous other cacti that have hallucinogenic properties. Among these are Doñana from northern Mexico, San Pedro from the Andes, three related mescaline-bearing species from South America, at least fifteen species used by the Indians of Central America, and at least fifteen species used by the Indians of Central Mexico as peyote substitutes. Botanists and chemists are now studying the constituents of these cacti and are making some remarkable discoveries.

In this book many of these cacti are examined, bringing the reader up to date on what scientists have learned about them so far. The various methods of ingestion are discussed. Techniques are presented for cultivating cacti and increasing the yield of mescaline and other alkaloids. There are descriptions of extracting mescaline mixed alkaloids from cacti. Also included is a brief discussion of the legal status of these entheogenic cacti and the names and addresses of suppliers from whom these plants/seeds can be obtained.

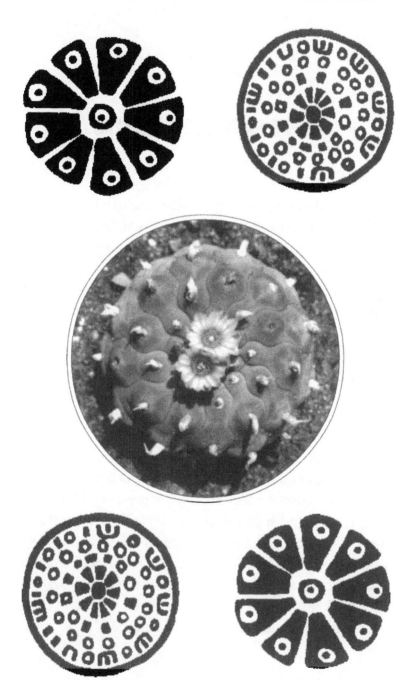

NATURAL POPULATIONS OF PEYOTE IN DECLINE

by Leonard Mercado

 Peyote is a native of the Chihuahan Desert (found specifically in portions of the Rio Grande Valley in Southern Texas and as far south as the state of San Luis Potosi in Mexico) and has been an item of commerce for a very long time. During the last 100 years it has been commercially harvested in the state of Texas, although its sale is now restricted by law to members of the Native American Church (NAC). It is estimated that the NAC has at least 250,000 members. The estimated annual harvest of individual plants, or buttons, is in the millions. When properly harvested, several new heads tend to form from the old root, thereby generating new plants for the future. Unfortunately, harvested plants are often cut deeply, leaving little or no root remaining in the ground.

In addition to commercial harvesting, large sections of the "peyote gardens" of Texas are uprooted to make room for new grazing land. Much of the small, slow-growing cacti such as peyote are destroyed as a result. Consequently, the regions where peyote may be found have greatly diminished. Areas where peyote once flourished in commercially harvestable quantities are now lacking this cactus entirely.

It is clear to us at The Peyote Foundation that the time to establish a conservation program is long overdue. While we encourage the preservation of peyote in its native habitat, we also feel it is the responsibility of those people who honor the divine cactus to grow it. This is a tangible way of establishing a close relationship with the plant, while helping to preserve the genetic diversity and well-being of the species.

We hope to establish a seed fund which will be used to purchase seeds from licensed peyote dealers. This seed will be propagated by The Peyote Foundation for eventual replanting in the wild or for future sacramental use. Eventually, Texas dealers might agree upon a means of allowing certain areas to be set aside for a period of time, unharvested, on a rotation basis. This would allow sufficient time for young peyotes to mature and establish stable populations. At the present, peyote is often harvested in an immature state.

The Peyote Foundation discourages continued non-sustainable harvesting in the wild. We do recommend that as much commercially harvested, fresh peyote as possible be re-rooted and cultivated rather than consumed. These plants will hopefully provide seeds and offsets for future generations.

Leonard Mercado is president of The Peyote Foundation, an organization devoted to protecting and promoting peyote and its spiritual paths.

MESCALINE, PEYOTE, AND THE LAW

by Richard Glen Boire, Esq.

 It was only about 100 years ago that the chemical mescaline was first isolated from the peyote cactus (*Lophophora williamsii*), and less than fifty years since Aldous Huxley related his first experience with synthetic mescaline sulfate in his book *The Doors of Perception*. Unfortunately, times have changed since Huxley ingested 250 milligrams of mescaline on a sunny spring morning in 1953.

Huxley broke no law by satisfying his intellectual curiosity about the intriguing substance. In our current "brave new world," however, investigations like Huxley's have been deemed crimes. Today we have lost control over our own minds; federal and state laws outlaw the possession of mescaline and peyote.

The first federal act to regulate mescaline went into effect in 1966.[1] In this same act, the federal government had the unmitigated arrogance to outlaw a natural living organism—the peyote cactus. Not much has changed since then. Today, both mescaline and peyote are included in Schedule I of the federal Controlled Substances Act; meaning that just about any act involving them is a federal crime punishable by prison time.

It's clear from the wording of the federal law, that the government would like to add peyote to the ever-lengthening list of extinct life-forms. Under federal law, peyote is defined as "all parts of the plant presently classified botanically as *Lophophora williamsii Lemaire,* whether growing or not, the seeds thereof, and extract from any part of such plant, and every compound, manufacture, salts, derivative, mixture, or preparation of such plant, its seeds or extracts." So, not only is it a federal crime just to possess a peyote cactus (dead or alive), but it's also a criminal act to plant peyote seeds, or even possess them.

The only explicit exception to the federal ban against possessing peyote pertains to members of the Native American Church (NAC). Under a federal regulation, NAC members are permitted to possess peyote so long as the peyote is for use "in bona fide religious ceremonies of the Native American Church." A 1994 federal act further expanded protection for Native American peyote users, by protecting all "Indians" (whether or not they are members of the Native Ameri-

---

[1] Largely out of racist motivations, by 1930 over a dozen states had already enacted laws outlawing the possession of peyote.

The earliest known law outlawing the ingestion of peyote was a product of the Spanish Inquisition. An edict issued in 1620 declared the ingestion of peyote to be an "act of superstition condemned as opposed to the purity and integrity of our Holy Catholic Faith. . ." (See Ramo de Inquisicion, tomo 289, Archivo General de la Nacion, Mexico City; quoted in Leonard, Irving A., "Decree Against Peyote, Mexican Inquisition, 1620." 44 *American Anthropologist* 324-336 (1942).

can Church), who use peyote in connection with the practice of a traditional Indian religion. The 1994 act protects qualifying Indians from *state* as well as federal prosecution.

Non-Native religious users of peyote who have sought a federal exemption similar to the one granted to Native American peyote users have been flatly rejected. Four states, however, have enacted statutory exemptions which protect *any* person who uses peyote for religious purposes. Oregon, for example, protects all religious users of peyote so long as they use it "in a manner that is not dangerous to the health of the user or others who are in the proximity of the user." Similar non-race based exemptions exist in Arizona, Colorado, and New Mexico. And, California and New York, while not having specific statutory exemptions, have court decisions on the books which recognize a religious

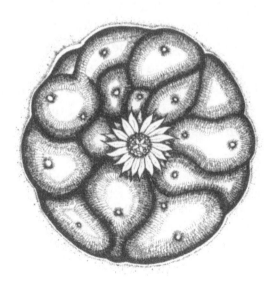

defense to peyote use. In these states, all sincere religious users of peyote should be able to invoke their state's religious exemption in the event of arrest for a personal amount of peyote. Even in these states, however, the religious use of *mescaline* remains a crime. Also, the *federal* government could still prosecute a religious user of peyote in the above states, because it is not bound by state laws.[2]

There is some good news. Aside from peyote, all the other cacti which endogenously produce mescaline (and there are over 20 species of such cacti), are not explicitly outlawed under federal and state drug laws. In other words, even high-mescaline-content cacti like *Trichocereus pachanoi*, *T. peruvianus*, and the others mentioned in this book, remain perfectly legal to possess and grow. This, however, did not stop California narcotics agents from raiding a *T. pachanoi* seller in 1987 and seizing and destroying thousands of pounds of living cacti. The nursery owner was charged with a gamut of crimes all stemming from the facts that the cacti naturally contained mescaline and the nursery owner had placed advertisements in counter-culture magazines. Charges were eventually dropped, but the man was nonetheless understandably traumatized by the whole

---

[2] Non-Native religious peyote users should be protected by the Religious Freedom Act of 1993 (RFRA). The details of RFRA are complex however, and cannot be adequately discussed in the limited space allotted this appendix. Therefore, I can do no more than call attention to RFRA's applicability to all religious peyote users.

experience, to say nothing of the financial imposition of the incident. (In addition to attorney's fees, he was forced to close his business.)

While it's patently absurd, it's always possible for an overzealous prosecutor to argue that all cacti which endogenously produce mescaline are illegal "mixtures" or "containers" of mescaline. This is the theory by which *Psilocybe* mushrooms have been ostensibly outlawed in a handful of states; as "containers" of the controlled substances psilocybin and psilocin. This ultra-reductionistic anthropocentric position outlaws any life-form that endogenously produces a substance which the government of the United States has controlled. No court has yet applied the theory to mescaline-producing cacti.

While mescaline-producing cacti other than peyote remain legal in the United States, a section of the federal law—that is repeated in most, if not all state laws—defines the crime of "manufacturing" a controlled substance so as to include extracting such a chemical "from substances of natural origin." While no court case has expressly addressed this issue with regard to cacti extractions, it is reasonable to assume that if a law enforcement agent ever found such an extraction (and recognized it), a prosecutor would use the provision to charge the person in possession of the extraction with manufacturing mescaline.

In other words, examination of the legal substrate underlying mescaline-producing cacti other than peyote, reveals a line separating the growing and possession of live cacti, from the extracting or otherwise processing of such cacti. Anyone who harvests their cacti and prepares it for ingestion, has moved from one side of this line to the other. Clearly, the current state of the law directs that it is unwise to process such cacti in amounts larger than can be consumed in the very near future. The difference between having a live *T. Pachanoi* growing in your home, and having a jug of pre-prepared tea, or capsules of powdered skin or flesh, could well be the difference between remaining a law abiding (and free) citizen and becoming a criminal.

With these notes in mind, I bid you welcome to the teachings which our cacti friends stand ready, willing, and able to share with anyone so interested.

Richard Glen Boire is a criminal defense attorney practicing in Northern California. He is the publisher of *The Entheogen Law Reporter* and the author of *Sacred Mushrooms and the Law* and *Marijuana Law*.

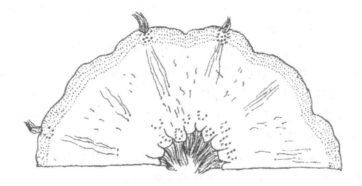

Peyote (latitudinal cross section)

NEW WORLD INQUISITION

Henceforth no person of whatever rank or social condition can or may make use of the said herb, Peyote, nor of any other kind under any name or appearance for the same or similar purposes, nor shall he make the Indians or any other person take them, with the further warning that disobedience to these decrees shall cause us, in addition to the penalties and condemnation above stated, to take action against such disobedient and recalcitrant persons as we would against those suspected of heresy to our Holy Catholic Faith.

—Licenciado D. Pedro Nabarre de Ysla, 1620

The protection of the Indians against the intoxication produced by the peyote or mescal button is a matter of supreme importance. Not only does it affect the obligation which the Government has toward its wards, but also particularly does it affect the physical, mental, and moral welfare of the Indians. . . .

The idea of making an intoxicating drug the basis of a religion is preposterous. One might as well use the sacrament as an excuse for drinking a gallon of wine to become intoxicated. This talk of religion is all a subterfuge. It is a bold attempt to perpetuate, under the guise of religion, the use of a drug that ought to be prohibited.

—U.S. Congressman Carl Hayden, 1937

EYOTE

(Lophophora williamsii)

 This spineless, tufted, blue-green, button-like cactus is the most famous of the entheogenic cacti. It grows wild from central Mexico to northern Texas. Its known history dates back to as early as 5000 B.C.

During the past two centuries the religious use of peyote spread northward into the United States and Canada among many of the Plains Indian tribes such as the Navajo, Comanche, Sioux, and Kiowa. This cactus eventually came to replace the hallucinogenic but dangerous red mescal bean *(Sophora secundiflora)* as a ceremonial sacrament. During the 1880's the North American peyote ritual was standardized. By 1920 the ceremonial practices of most tribes were identical with only minor variations.

It was in 1896 that Arthur Heffter extracted mescaline from peyote and tested it upon himself. This was the first hallucinogenic compound ever to be isolated. About 350 milligrams of mescaline is required for a entheogenic experience, although definite effects can be felt from as little as 100 milligrams. Mescaline may comprise as much as six percent of the weight of the dried button but is more often closer to one percent. An average dried button the diameter of a quarter weighs about two grams. It usually takes six to ten of these buttons to gain the desired effect.

It has often been noted that the peyote experience is qualitatively somewhat different than that of pure mescaline, the former being more physical than the latter. This is due to several of the other alkaloids present in the cactus. These include: hordenine, N-methylmescaline, N-acetylmescaline, pellotine, anhalinine, anhalonine, anhalidine, anhalonidine, anahalamine, O-methylanhalonidine, tyramine, and lophophorine. Not all of these substances exhibit psychopharmacological activity when administered singly. Some of them in combination apparently potentiate the effects of the mescaline and definitely alter some characteristics of the experience.

Two of these alkaloids—hordenine and tyramine—have been found to possess antibacterial properties, presumably because of their phenolic function. For ages the Huichol Indians have rubbed the juices of fresh peyote into wounds to prevent infection and promote healing. The Tarahumara Indians consume small amounts of peyote to combat hunger, thirst, and exhaustion—especially while hunting. They have been known to run for days after a deer without food, water, or rest. Peyote has many uses in traditional medicine, including the treatment of arthritis, consumption, influenza, intestinal disorders, diabetes, snake and scorpion bites, and datura poisoning.

The Huichol and other tribes recognize two forms of peyote. One is larger, more potent, and more bitter than the other. They call it *tzinouritehua-hikuri* (peyote of gods). The smaller, more palatable but milder buttons are called *rhaitoumuanitari-hikuri* (peyote of goddesses). The difference between the two forms may be due solely to how old the plants are. Alkaloids tend to accumulate in these cacti with age. It is possible, however, that the goddess peyote is a different species. Until recently, botanists believed that the genus *Lophophora* consisted of a single but highly variable species. But in 1967 H.H. Bravo found near Queretaro in south-central Mexico another species which he named *L. diffusa*. This plant is yellow-green, soft, and ribless and contains a somewhat different alkaloid mixture with far less mescaline than *L. williamsii*.

Peyote of Goddesses and Peyote of Gods

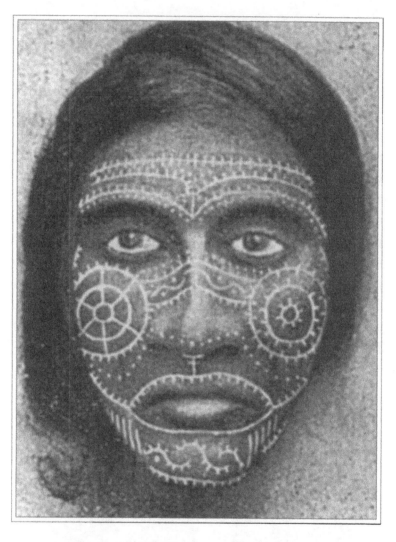

Speak to the Peyote with your heart, with your thoughts.
And the Peyote sees your heart. . . .
And if you have luck, you will hear things and receive things
that are invisible to others,
but that God has given you to pursue your path.

—from a Huichol novice shaman

ᵀHE EXPERIENCE

 About half an hour after ingesting the buttons, the first effects are felt. There is a feeling of strange intoxication and shifting consciousness with minor perceptual changes. There may also be strong physical effects, including respiratory pressure, muscular tension (especially in the face and neck muscles), and queasiness or possible nausea. Any unpleasant sensations should disappear within an hour.

After this, the state of altered consciousness begins to manifest itself. The experience may vary with the individual, but among the possible occurrences are feelings of inner tranquillity, oneness with life, heightened awareness, and rapid thought flow. During the next several hours these effects will deepen and become more visual. Colors may become more intense. Halos or auras may appear about things. Objects may seem larger, smaller, closer, or more distant than they actually are. Persons will often notice little or no changes in visual perception while beholding the world about them, but upon closing their eyes they will see on their mind-screen wildly colorful and constantly changing patterns.

After several more hours the intensity of the experience gradually relaxes. Thought becomes less rapid and diffuse and more ordered. In the Navajo peyote ritual this change of thought flow is used wisely. During the first part of the ceremony, the participants submit to the feeling and let the peyote teach them. During the latter part of the ritual, the mind turns to thoughtful contemplation, and understanding with the conscious intellect what the peyote has taught the subconscious spirit.

The entire experience may last from six to twelve hours, depending upon the individual and the amount of the plant consumed. After all of the peyote effects have passed, there is no come-down. One is likely to feel pleasantly relaxed and much at peace with the world. Although there is usually no desire for food during the experience, one will probably have a wholesome appetite afterwards.

I was
seeing what Adam
had seen on the morn-
ing of his creation—the
miracle, moment by
moment, of naked
existence.

—from *The Doors of Perception*
by Aldous Huxley

Methods of Use

 The most common method of use is simply to chew up and swallow the fresh or dried buttons after removing the tufts and sand. This is the way it is almost always done at Indian ceremonies. Most people find the taste of this cactus unbearably bitter. The Indians, however, believe that if one's heart is pure, the bitterness will not be tasted. Many have found that by not cringing from the taste but rather by letting one's senses plunge directly into the center of the bitterness, a sort of separation from the offensive flavor is experienced. One is aware of the bitterness, but it is no longer disturbing. This is similar to the practice of bringing one's consciousness to the center of pain, so that detachment may occur. It is not a difficult trick, but it takes some mental discipline.

People who cannot endure the bitterness of peyote often go to various extremes to get it into the system without having to taste it. One fairly effective method is to drink unsweetened grapefruit juice while chewing it. The acids in the juice somewhat neutralize some of the bitter bases.

Another method is to grind the buttons in a pepper grinder and pack the pulverized material in 000 capsules, which are then washed down with warm water. This is an effective method, but it can take 20 capsules or more to get a 350 milligram dose of mescaline.

People often will boil the buttons in water for several hours to make a very concentrated tea. A cup of this decoction can be swallowed in a few hasty gulps.

Another preparation that is occasionally used is a Jell-O™ type dessert made with the fresh or dried plant. If spoonfuls are swallowed whole, the gelatin serves as a sort of shield protecting the tastebuds from contact with the bitter material. It also slows down the absorption of the drug in the digestive tract. This can be of value.

IExperts recommend that anyone consuming peyote or mescaline ingest it gradually during a period of an hour or take two half-doses 45 minutes apart. This is done to reduce the shock of the alkaloids on the system. Nausea or queasiness is sometimes experienced half an hour or so after using peyote or mescaline. This usually passes in less than an hour. A sip of grapefruit juice will sometimes dispel the sick feeling.

During the peyote ceremony Indians encourage vomiting rather than trying to hold it in. Throwing up, they believe, is a purging of both physical and spiritual ills. Most tribes fast for at least a day before taking peyote. This can also help to minimize gastric distress. One should not eat for at least six hours before taking either mescaline or peyote.

A controversial method which avoids both the bitterness and the nausea is the rectal infusion, or enema. Caution is required with enemas to avoid infection, transmission of disease, and other potential problems. 8-16 grams of dried peyote are ground to a fine powder and boiled in a pint of water for 30 minutes. The resulting tea is then strained and further boiled to reduce its volume to 1/2 pint. After cooling, this is taken as an enema using a small bulb syringe and retained for at least two hours. If there is any fecal matter in the lower bowel, a small cleansing enema can be taken and thoroughly expelled before having the peyote infusion. Otherwise, much of the drug may be taken up by the feces and later voided.

Some people enjoy the effects of smoking peyote. They grind it well and combine it with marijuana or other herbs. The odor and taste of burning peyote is not as pleasant as that of cannabis. Also, the effect is remarkably subtle. It adds an interesting quality to the cannabis high, but the entheogenic experience does not occur. There is no nausea from smoking peyote.

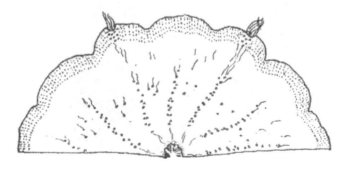

Peyote (latitudinal cross section)

from Barbabra Meyerhoff: Peyote Hunt: The Sacred Journey of the Huichol Indians

Huichol shaman

𝕱INDING AND 𝕻ICKING 𝕻EYOTE

The peyote cactus may be found in many areas throughout the Chihuahuan Desert from central Mexico to southern Texas. Sometimes it grows in open sunlit places, but more often it is found in clusters under fairly large shrubs, among mesquite or creosote bushes, or in the shade of larger succulents. During the last twenty years, however, peyote has become extremely scarce in its native habitat due to overharvesting.

The best time to harvest any cactus is after a long dry spell. The worst time is during or after a rainy period. The plants build up alkaloids during dry seasons and draw upon them for growth when the rains come. If the plants are harvested during or after a wet spell, the alkaloid content may have dropped below fifty percent. Also, freshly cut plants will rot if exposed to the rain. A soil test kit can provide a good indication of the potency of wild cacti. If the soil is rich in nitrogen, the plants are likely to be rich in alkaloids.

When harvesting peyote, many people uproot the entire plant. This is unnecessary and wasteful. The roots contain no mescaline. Some of these plants have taken a long time to reach their size. A cactus three inches in diameter may be more than twenty years old. To collect peyote properly, the button is be cleanly decapitated slightly above ground level. When the roots are left intact, new buds will form where the old one was removed. These will eventually develop into full-size buttons, which may be harvested as before. If the new heads are not allowed to reach full size and flower, however, no seedlings will be produced and eventually the roots will expire. Faulty harvesting methods have seriously depleted populations of this cactus.

Because of the presence of several phenolic alkaloids, peyote cacti do not spoil easily and may be kept in their fresh form for up to a year after harvesting if they are not damaged. Bruised plants, however, will rot quickly. Some shrinkage and drying out due to water loss is normal and will not effect the potency of the peyote. If they are to be kept longer than this, the cacti must be dried. The enzymes which cause the harvested plant to ultimately decompose also destroy the mescaline and other alkaloids. To dry peyote buttons, they are laid out in the hot sun or in an oven at 250° F until completely devoid of moisture.

HUNTING THE PEYOTE

Once a year, the Huichols make a sacred trip to gather Hikuri [peyote]. The trek is led by an experienced *mara'akame* or shaman, who is in contact with Tatewari (Our grandfather-fire). Tatewari is the oldest Huichol god, also known as Hikuri, the Peyote-god. He is personified with Peyote plants on his hands and feet, and he interprets all the deities to the modern shamans, often through visions, sometimes indirectly through Kauyumari (the Sacred Deer Person and culture hero). Tatewari led the first Peyote pilgrimage far from the present area inhabited by the nine thousand Huichols into Wirikuta, an ancestral region where Peyote abounds. Guided by the shaman, the participants, usually ten to fifteen in number, take on the identity of deified ancestors as they follow Tatewari "to find their life."

—from *Plants of the Gods* by Richard Evans Schultes and Albert Hofmann

Mexico represents without a doubt the world's richest area in diversity and use of hallucinogens in aboriginal societies. . .[In addition to Peyote] . . . other cactus species are still used in northern Mexico as minor hallucinogens for special magico-religious purposes.

—from *Plants of the Gods* by
Richard Evans Schultes and Albert Hofmann

ᛞTHER ᛞACTI ᛞF ᛞENTRAL ᛞEXICO

 There are several cacti which are used by the Tarahumara and other tribes of central Mexico as substitutes for peyote. Many of these cacti are now under investigation for their alkaloidal content and psychopharmacological activity. Progress is somewhat retarded in the studies of the effects of these plants, because almost all experimentation has been conducted upon laboratory animals rather than humans. Some of these cacti have been found to contain mescaline and other related alkaloids with known sympathomimetic properties. Much further research, however, is needed on these plants and their activity.

Peyotillo *(Pelecyphora aselliformis)*

This small cactus is known sometimes as "hatchet cactus" because of its oddly flattened tubercules. It is often found growing in the state of San Luis Potosi in central Mexico. The plant contains traces of mescaline too minute to have any effect. It also contains small amounts of anhalidine; anhaladine; hordenine; N-methyl-

Tsuwiri

Sunami

mescaline; pellotine; 3-demethyltrichocereine; B-phenethylamine; N-methyl-B-phenethylamine; 3,4-dimethoxy-B-phenethylamine; N-methyl-3,4-dimethoxy-B-phenethylamine; and 4-methoxy-B-phenethylamine. Most of these are also found in peyote but in much larger quantities.

Tsuwiri *(Ariocarpus retusus)*

The Huichol name *tsuwiri* means "false peyote." These people make long pilgrimages to sacred places in search of the peyote that grows there. They believe that if a person has not been properly purified, the spirits will lead him to the "false peyote" and that if he partakes of it, he will suffer madness or at least a bad trip. The plant is known among some tribes as *chautle* or *chaute*. These names are also used for other *Ariocarpus* species. This cactus contains hordenine and N-methyltyramine in fairly small amounts (about 0.02% each) and traces of N-methyl-3,4-dimethoxy-B-phenethylamine and N-methyl-4-B-phenethylamine. Aside from these alkaloids, it also contains a flavone called retusin (3',3',4',7-tetramethoxy-5-hydroxyflavone). Although alkaloid content may vary some at different seasons or stages of growth, from the scientific point of view, the amounts present in this plant appear insufficient to produce any psychopharmacological response.

Sunami

Doñana

Sunami *(Ariocarpus fissuratus)*

This plant has been long used in the traditional medicine of Mexico and the southwestern USA. It is believed to be more potent than peyote and is used in the same manner or made into an intoxicating drink. Among some tribes it is known as *chaute* (a generic name for the *Ariocarpus* species), living rock, or dry whiskey. The latter name, however, is often also used for peyote and other entheogenic cacti. There are two varieties of *A. fissuratus: var. lloydii* and *var. fissuratus*. Both have about the same phytochemical makeup. The plant contains mostly hordenine, less N-methyltyramine, and some N-methyl-3,4-dimethoxy-B-phenethylamine. There are two other species that also contain these alkaloids—*A. kotschoubeyanus* (also known as *pata de venado* or *pezuna de venado*) and *A. trigonus*.

Doñana *(Coryphantha macromeris)*

This small cactus from northern Mexico has been found to contain macromerine, a phenethylamine drug reputed to have about 1/5 the potency of mescaline. It also contains: normacromerine; N-formylnormacromerine; tyramine; N-methyltyramine; hordenine; N-methyl-3,4-dimethoxy-B-phenethylamine; metanephrine; and synephrine (a macromerine precursor).

Doñana

Dolichothele

Other *Coryphantha* species that contain macromerine along with most of these other alkaloids include: *C. pectinada, C. elephantideus, C. runyonii,* and *C. cornifera var. echinus.* Most of these alkaloids, with the exception of macromerine, have also been found in other varieties of *C. cornifera* and in *C. durangensis, C. ottonis, C. poselgeriana,* and *C. ramillosa.*

Considering that there is usually no more than 0.1% macromerine in Doñana and that a gram or more of this alkaloid may be needed to produce an entheic effect, one would have to consume more than a kilo of the dried cactus or twenty pounds of the fresh plant. Clearly this is not possible for most humans. If one wishes to experiment with the hallucinogenic properties of Doñana, it is necessary first to make an extraction of the mixed alkaloids. Methods for this are described later.

Dolichothele

Several tribes occasionally use any one of several species of *Dolichothele* as a peyote-like sacrament. These include *D. baumii, D. longimamma, D. melalenca, D. sphaerica, D. surculosa,* and *D. uberiformis.* Recent investigations have revealed in these the presence of small amounts of the following alkaloids: N-methylphenethylamine; B-O-methylsynephrine; N-methyltryramine; synephrine; hordenine; and dolichotheline (N-isovaleryhistamine).

Obregonia denegrii

Astrophytum asterias

Miscellaneous

Several other cacti are used by the Tarahumara as peyote substitutes. Among these are *Obregonia denegrii, Aztekium ritterii, Astrophytum asterias, A. capricorne, A. myriostigma* (Bishop's Cap), and *Solisia pectinata*. The Tarahumara also consume a cactus which they call *mulato (Mammillaria micromeris)* and claim it prolongs life, gives speed to runners, and clarifies vision for mystical insights. Another cactus similarly employed is known as *rosapara (Epitheliantha micromeris)* and is believed by many botanists to be the same species as *mulato*, but at a later vegetative stage. The large cactus *Pachycereus pecten-aboriginum*, known locally as *cawe*, is occasionally used as a narcotic.

What little studies have been carried out on these cacti have revealed the presence of alkaloids found in most of the other species already discussed, but not the presence of mescaline or macromerine. Many of these alkaloids have some psychopharmacological properties, but nothing to compare with those of mescaline and macromerine. Furthermore, the amounts of these alkaloids are usually so small as to be insignificant. For example, the species *Obregonia denegrii* contains tyramine 0.003%, hordenine 0.002%, and N-methyltyramine 0.0002%. These are all known sympathomimetics, but the percentages are far too minute to have any value. Several publications in recent years have mentioned the sacramental use of

Aztekium ritterii

Bishop's Cap

these cacti. As a result thousands of people have obtained these plants from cactus dealers and ingested them, usually with disappointing (and sometimes nauseating) results. Sadly, many of these cacti are quite rare. If too many people destroy them experimentally, they may become seriously endangered species. The most suitable cacti for a true psychedelic experience are peyote (which is for the most part illegal and on the verge of extinction) and the several species of *Trichocereus* such as San Pedro (which are legal and easy to obtain and cultivate).

> The Tarahumare
> designate several [cacti]
> as *hikuli*. . . . These plants
> live for months after they
> have been rooted up, and the
> eating of them causes a state of
> ecstasy. They are, therefore,
> considered demi-gods, who
> have to be treated with
> great reverence. . . .

> —from *Unknown Mexico*
> by C. Lumhultz

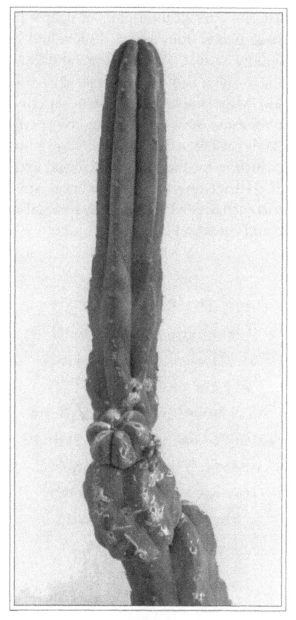

San Pedro

SAN PEDRO

(Trichocereus pachanoi)

 This plant is native to the Andes of Peru and Ecuador. Unlike the small peyote cactus, San Pedro is large and multi-branched. In its natural environment it often grows to heights of ten to fifteen feet. Its mescaline content is less than that of peyote (0.3%-1.2%), but because of its great size and rapid growth, it may provide a more economical source of mescaline than peyote. In addition, it makes more ecological sense to use the more easily grown and abundant San Pedro than the endangered peyote.

San Pedro also contains tyramine; hordenine; 3-methoxytyramine; anhalaninine; anhalonidine; 3,4-dimethoxyphenethylamine; 3,4-dimethoxy-4-hydroxy-B-phenethylamine; and 3,5-dimethoxy-4-hydroxy-B-phenethylamine. Some of these are known sympathomimetics. Others have no apparent effects when ingested by themselves. It is possible, however, that in combination with mescaline and the other active compounds they may produce a synergistic effect. It is also possible that any compounds in the plant which act as mild MAO inhibitors will render a person vulnerable to some of the above-mentioned amines, which ordi-

San Pedro

Drying San Pedro

narily must be metabolized before they take effect.

The effects of San Pedro are in many ways more pleasant than those of peyote. To begin with, its taste is only slightly bitter, and the initial nausea is not as likely to occur. When the full entheogenic experience takes hold, it is less overwhelming, more tranquil, and not nearly as physical as that of peyote.

San Pedro can be eaten fresh or dried or taken in any of the manners described for peyote. Cuttings of San Pedro sold in the USA are usually about three feet long and four inches in diameter. A piece six inches long is the usual recommended dose. Many people have reported that this doesn't quite produce the desired effects. For a real mind opening experience, a piece at least one foot long has been recommended. The skin and the spines must be removed. The skin should not be thrown away, however. The green tissue close to the skin contains a high concentration of mescaline. Some people chew the skin until all of the juices are extracted. Or the skins can be boiled in water for several hours to make a potent tea. The woody core of the cactus cannot be eaten. One can eat around it like a corn cob. The core does not have much alkaloid content but can be mashed and boiled as a tea for what little is there.

To dry San Pedro, the cactus is sliced into disks (actually stars) 1/2 inch thick and dried thoroughly in the sun or in an oven at 250° F. The spines must be removed either before drying or before chewing. Also, one must be careful of the splinters from the woody core.

T. peruvianus

If a tea is to be made from fresh San Pedro, the cactus must be either sliced, chopped, or crushed before boiling.

San Pedro is a hardy cactus and endures cold climates quite well. It grows at altitudes from sea level to 9000 feet high in the Andes, where it is most frequently found on western slopes. The soil in this region is very rich in humus and various minerals. This helps in the production of mescaline and other alkaloids.

There are several cacti which look like San Pedro and have even been mistaken for it by trained botanists. In 1960 when Turner and Heyman discovered that San Pedro contained mescaline, they erroneously identified the plant as *Opuntia cylindrica*. A few other South American species of *Trichocereus* also contain mescaline and related alkaloids. These include: *T. bridgesii, T. macrogonus, T. terscheckii,* and *T. werdermannianus.*

There is evidence that the ritualistic use of San Pedro dates back to 1000 B.C. Even today it is used by the *curanderos* (medicine men) of northern Peru. They prepare a drink called *cimora* from it and take this in a ceremonial setting to diagnose the spiritual (or subconscious) basis of a patient's illness.

Recently, *Trichocereus peruvianus* has gained some favor as a more potent cousin of San Pedro. This species resembles San Pedro in form except for a lighter blue color and awesome three to four inch thorns. *T. peruvianus* is purported to contain ten times the mescaline content of San Pedro (i.e. approximately the same content as peyote).

Derek K. Westlund

Home Peyote Graden

CULTIVATION OF PEYOTE AND OTHER CACTI

by Derek K. Westlund

 The following five sections were written by Derek K. Westlund, a *Lophophora* cultivation researcher and author who currently publishes *Peyotl: The Medicine Journal.* He is also an associate member of The Peyotl Way Church of God and was a Founding Officer of The Peyote Foundation, serving as the first Chief Curator.

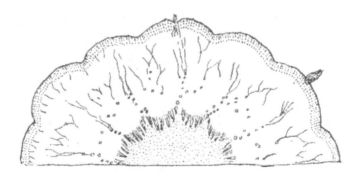

Peyote (latitudinal cross section)

Derek K. Westlund

Home Cacti Garden

ℹNTRODUCTION AND ℰNVIRONMENT

Since it is basically illegal for anyone other than bona fide peyotists to possess *Lophophora*, there is very little in the way of reputable research on this genus. All previous research has been conducted on field collected plants, leaving peyote cultivation an extremely obscure topic. It is true that in the desert peyote grows extremely slow, but contrary to popular belief peyote can be easily cultivated at home. And with a little extra attention its rate of growth can be markedly increased.

Standard cacti cultivation methods have taken great leaps since this book was first published. Experimentation, ingenuity, and simple trial and error has lead to the discovery that most cacti respond incredibly well to liberal feedings, high heat, and an abundance of water. Nurserymen can now easily grow peyote from seed to flowering plant in three years or less. Using a rotating system of seed growing, grafting, and re-rooting, a full blown, self-sustaining peyote garden can be established in just two to three years. Peyote can even be cultivated indoors.

For best results some type of greenhouse is built. Proper heat and lighting is critical for cacti. During the summer a 50-65% shade cloth is necessary on the roof and west side. In the winter only the south face should be shaded. The greenhouse should be positioned so that it gets the longest day possible. No matter what type of cacti is growing, shade screening will always produce more lush, healthy plant tissue. Something with a corrugated fiberglass roof or a PVC/poly quonset hut is sufficient to achieve decent results. Waist level benches and a water source also makes things really nice. A southern facing back porch or window sill may be adequate.

This nursery will protect and provide for the plants in many ways. Creating the proper atmosphere is not difficult. Many cacti can survive below freezing, but not for long, especially when it is frosty. Most don't even reach optimal growing temperature until it hits around 100°. Expert cactii growers keep the greenhouse or home warm, some read up on greenhouse mechanics and get it hot, about 110°. Most cacti, including *Lophophora*, can be heavily watered and liberally fertilized throughout the summer months. Misting reduces extreme heat and provides humidity simultaneously, but it isn't good for cactti to allow any pots to remain soaked during really hot spells (over 110°), because the roots will "boil." It is both easier and more enjoyable to water plants than repair or replace damaged ones. The grafting techniques presented later will give you a much greater margin for error.

Growing Peyote and Other Cacti from Seed

 Peyote can be propagated by a variety of methods. Transplanting live plants, taking cuttings, and grafting are just a few, but the most determined seekers will discover that growing peyote from seed is their last resort. Although most of the literature produced on peyote over the last few decades referred to plants growing in their natural habitat, recently it has been discovered that peyote grows quite quickly in a controlled environment, so one doesn't have to wait a generation to harvest.

Organic Methods or Fungicide

There are probably just as many techniques for seed germination as there are ways to propagate adult plants. The method chosen will depend on personal preferences and available resources. For people who are not disturbed by using fungicide, just about any soil will suffice; for those who are strict organic gardeners, a micro-hydroponic system is the key.

Persons willing to use fungicides will discover that a little sacrifice of purity will allow a faster and easier start than the strictly organic method. Fungicide, when used properly will not only eliminate *damp off* (saving perhaps the entire batch), but it will also allow the peyote seedlings to grow unchecked; maintaining a uniform and steady growth up through the plantlet stage. Fortunately, non-systemic fungicides are never absorbed by the plant itself. Even those brands of fungicide that are absorbed into the plant have plenty of time to break down or be expelled, since the fungicide is only necessary for the first four months of growth.

Some people think that baking the soil kills all micro organisms in the medium, thus providing a perfectly safe environment. This is only true to a certain extent. When fresh air is introduced to the system spores and insects come in contact with the soil and contaminate it anyway. The seed germination area provides an excellent environment for pests to flourish. Once algae, mold, and bugs start to live and breed in the containers they are very hard to eliminate. The peyote seedlings are lost, unless a chemical pesticide/fungicide is used (possibly at a greater strength than would have been needed to prevent the occurrence in the first place).

When the organic/hydroponic method is used, it is important to minimize the organic components in the soil by creating an inert medium (consisting of sand and perlite) and then fertilizing with an organically derived, water soluble plant food that is full of trace minerals. When applied sparingly between regular waterings, the peyote is nourished, but nothing else has time to become established.

Regardless of which of these method is used, humidity is a necessity for cacti seedlings and humidity promotes all of the previously mentioned pests.

Soil Mixtures

There are many combinations possible when making peyote soil. Sand, peat, lime stone, blood meal, bone meal, potting soil, bat guano, rabbit shit, vermiculite, perilite, and polymers are commonly used components. It doesn't really make much difference what is used, as long as none of the components create any extreme condition, such as nitrogen burn, saline dehydration, or mud.

Some of the best results have been achieved by accident, using the simplest of materials. However, most people prefer to have an exact recipe. The following recipe has been tested and found to work well.

Soil Mixture Formula

$^1/_3$ *fine, washed silica sand (similar to beach sand),*
$^1/_3$ *screened peat,* $^1/_3$ *perlite*
are mixed together and put in $3 \, ^1/_4''$ *x* $3 \, ^1/_4''$ *x* $4''$ *pots,*
leaving $^1/_2''$ *of space at the top of the pots.*

New material is used, and enough mixture is made to fill an entire flat of pots. If there aren't enough peyote seeds to do a whole flat, the "false peyote" is growm in the extra space. Peyote loves companion plants and will respond positively to the surrounding life force.

Planting the Seeds

It doesn't matter what time of year the seeds are sown, because the seedlings can be incorporated into any reasonable environment by giving them enough time to adapt. The cacti seed are placed directly on the surface of the soil, and a top dressing of sand is lightly sprinkled over the area. The pots are set in a shallow bowl of tepid water, and the moisture is allowed to soak throughout. The hydroponic method uses a mixture of clean fish tank gravel, sand, and perlite. Care should be taken not to lose the seeds in the gaps between the pebbles. To prevent this, a top dressing of sand is sprinkled on the mixture and misted before the seeds are placed. Then the seeds are placed and sprinkled with sand as previously described. Now instead of the container being soaked in a bowl of water, the surface is misted until it is soaked deep through.

Germination

After all of the containers are planted, they are put back in the flat. The flat is then stored in a place that will stay 90° during the day and 60° at night. If possible, the temperature should be maintained at a constant 80°.

This special place should receive heavily screened sunlight or fluorescent light. The ideal amount of light is 16-18 hours. Direct sunlight will damage even mature peyote plants, so the use of shade cloth is absolutely critical. For seedlings, 65% or greater should be used, depending on if there is a layer of poly or fiberglass further diffusing the light. On the other hand, not enough light will cause spindly elongated growth. All in all, slightly more light is better than slightly less light.

No matter which method is used, humidity must be maintained at 60-90% by building a terrarium, covering each pot with a perforated sandwich bag, or occasionally misting as needed. Persons using soil can continue bottom watering or adopt a misting schedule.

Seedlings

The seeds will germinate in three to ten days. Initially they'll appear as little green balls, but a trained eye will soon notice the cotyledons and first set of areoles (the growth tip, identifiable by locating a spine). With the soil method, the peyote will be able to draw nutrients directly from the medium; this should be plenty of food for the first four to five months. Fungicide is added to the mist bottle and applied only when needed. With the hydro-method, misting will be the only practical way to water. Fungicide shouldn't be necessary, but feeding will have to be supplemented with a specialty fertilizer. The best choice would be an organically derived, water soluble, hydroponic fertilizer, low in nitrogen and full of trace elements. A good one is Ion 2000™ from Arbico in Arizona. Miracle Grow™ makes a low nitrogen variety that would work fine, but it has added color (a strength indicator) that will stain your medium.

The seedlings are allowed to grow like this for about six months, then their environment is made drier, hotter, and brighter. The waterings will become deeper and less frequent. If a green house is available, they may be placed there, but extra shading should be used for a little longer. For those living in the desert, the best time to sow seed and adapt seedlings to the green house is in the winter. This is mainly because it is easier to control the environment at this time.

Transplanting

Peyote doesn't mind being crowded and actually seems to prefer it. They could be transplanted after six months, but don't need too until they're really cramped or the soil appears to be accumulating to many "salts." Cacti will respond well to transplanting, but as a general rule, if they're growing steadily, they should be left alone.

Transplanting is quite easy. The pot is simply inverted onto the palm of your hand and the soil is gently washed away with a garden hose until one's hand is full of little tiny seedlings. The roots are allowed to almost completely dry out. This takes one or two days. After more soil has been prepared, the little peyote is suspended with fingers or padded tweezers while the other hand fills the pot around the plant. It is possible to poke a hole in the soil and drop the peyote in place, but only if the medium is dry. The plantlets can be adjusted a bit, so long as the roots and soil are completely dry. After they have sat undisturbed for a few more days, a regular watering schedule is gradually introduced. Within a matter of days the plants should plump up.

Peyote is self-pollinating and will flower in its third year. If one starts out by grafting some six month old seedlings, it is possible to get flowers that produce viable seeds about six to twelve months later. Within the second year of cultivatiion it is possible to obtain a steady supply of seeds and off-shoots, and possibly enough material to consider ingesting.

GROWING CACTI FROM CUTTINGS AND MAKING GRAFT STOCK

 Cacti can easily be propagated by removing a healthy limb and rooting it. Most cacti, including *Lophophora*, will produce off-sets when the main plant reaches maturity. Occasionally, these will already have tiny roots where the pup touched the soil. Although it is necessary to allow time for the exposed tissue to callous, the pre-rooted heads take off quickly. This plant is essentially a clone and, once established, could flower along with the mother plant, thus providing more seed.

By taking cuttings one can quickly produce uniform graft stock, further propagate rare plants and expand their seed bank. If the goal is speed, growing graft stock from seed is literally a waste of time, unless there is no other alternative. Columnar cacti seedlings will often topple, because they taper down at the base where the circumference is still seedling size. This is just one of the many reasons not to graft onto seed grown plants.

The top portion of a young columnar can be cut off and rooted to provide an excellent graft stock or specimen. The piece that was left in the pot or ground will almost always produce new growth, unless all of the areoles were removed. On a rare cactus such as peyote, plenty of clearly visible areoles should be left on the mother plant. Taking a cutting off the top of a peyote that doesn't have a large enough tap root could kill it. If this is the case, only the pups should be removed.

After the selected piece is sliced off, it is immediately dipped in root hormone powder. If there is a chance the peyote will be eaten at some later date, consideration is given to what the cutting is dipped into. The cut should be completely cauterized (this will drastically reduce dehydration of *Myrtillo* cacti). If the cuttings are going to be used for graft stock, as many as possible are made. For columnar cacti, the cuttings should be set in a flat and placed in a more shady area. Most peyote-shaped cacti can be inverted while healing to allow the cut to dry more quickly.

The excess root hormone powder is rinsed off twenty-four hours later. A thin, almost translucent skin should be noticeable. If the hormone is left on too long, it could continue to draw moisture from the cutting, dehydrating it while forming a thick scab. These conditions will inhibit root growth. If conditions are optimal, the cuttings are misted on a daily basis. If its cooler in the garden, the cuttings are allowed to sit dry. Eventually, roots will be visible beneath the treated area. Once they break free, the cutting may be potted.

The cacti is placed in completely dry soil, in a manner that gives the base enough support without burying too much of the stem. Small peyote buttons can be planted so the top is flush with the soil. *Myrtillo* cactus should be set on the surface and just sprinkled with soil around the edges; San Pedro and other columnar cacti are happy around one inch down. The cutting is placed in a pot that isn't too large, because the cutting won't be drinking much for a while. At first, only evaporation will be removing moisture from the soil. The plant should be watered lightly until new growth is clearly evident. Care should be taken not to jostle the plants.

Some cacti, like *Myrtillocactus* and *Lophophora*, react quite well to this method of propagation. Many cacti in this book, such as *Ariocarpus*, take a long time to root and may rot. *Aztekium* simply will not root up; they must be grafted or grown from seed. All the cacti cuttings need a low nitrogen, high phosphorous fertilizer to stimulate further root development and proper tissue consistency. Although high nitrogen will dramatically increase growth rate, the cacti will swell, split and/or become hollow. During the fall and winter these plants will have a lower survival rate because they'll be unable to "harden off" against the cold.

Derek K. Westlund

Three-month-old grafts

GRAFTING PEYOTE AND OTHER CACTI

 An astonishing breakthrough in cacti cultivation is tissue grafting. This technical sounding procedure is actually very easy and extremely advantageous to the production nurseryman. If one knows a little about plants and has some form of peyote, (a seed, an offshoot, or even a fresh wedge), one could get started immediately, indoors or out.

Graft Stock

All that is necessary is some *Myrtillocactus geometrizan*, also known as the Blue Myrtle. San Pedro or any other spine-free, hardy columnar will do. Experts use myrtillo because they like its characteristics. These are going to be the graft stock. Compared to peyote, they grow very quickly and are more water tolerant. In the choosing of graft stock there is a debate over possible alkaloidal exchange between stock (myrtillo) and scion (peyote). San Pedro produces mescaline, myrtillo doesn't. I don't think it matters much which you use in that regard, because the alkaloids don't flow.

San Pedro, however, are slippery to graft onto. Some *Trichocereus* get black rot easily (especially where cut), and all are susceptible to pyrethrene burn (pyretherine is an organic pesticide), whereas myrtillo is not. Pre-rooted, ready to go stocks can be bought or self-produced by rooting cuttings. The stock plant should be at least 4 to 6 inches tall and $^3/_4$ to 1 inch in diameter; the larger the better. The pot must be proportionate to the plant, so that the soil can go through wet and dry spells. For faster, more uniform results, root hormone, a well draining cacti mix, and uniform plastic pots that fit in a flat are used.

Grafting the Scion Onto the Stock

In the warm months the graft stock (perhaps hundreds) will be actively growing in perfect harmony with the proposed *Lophophora*. Peyote can be grafted before it's even a $^1/_4$ inch in diameter. One should have a flat razor-sharp knife, a means to clean and sharpen it, and some pre-stretched, household rubber bands. The two cacti tissues are going to be sliced and grafted together. It must always be kept in mind that this is strictly for production reasons. One should never sacrifice this medicine with other than the best intentions.

The stocks are pre-watered. One is chosen with a diameter near to that of the scion. The top one-third of the obviously fresher growth on the myrtillo is sliced off. Actively growing tissue is needed, so some fresh growth must remain on the stock. The areoles (spined area) near the tip are beveled down, with as little disturbance to the side tissue as possible. The result is a blunt ended "pencil" shape. Now a thin layer is carefully sliced off the bottom of the scion (peyote) to produce a perfectly circular, flat surface. The tippy top of the stock is quickly sliced off once more to produce the utmost perfect surface.

These two diameters are made as close in size as possible. If necessary, they are resliced. The button is placed on the top of the stock with the center tissues carefully lined up. It doesn't matter in which order the cuts are made, but they must be done quickly. A natural adhesion will hold everything in place long enough for gentle placement of a rubber band around the pot, stock, and scion, with another crisscrossing the first. This applies equal pressure everywhere, not too tight but quickly. If necessary, the stock and scion are realigned. The tension of the rubberbands should be mostly on the pot not the button.

Caring for the Fresh Grafts

The fresh grafts are set in a dimmer, cooler place for the first day, then placed back with the rest for the second day. When conditions are optimal, the two tissues will start to fuse instantly, losing almost no growth time. If left undisturbed, healing will occur in just days. On the third day, the rubberbands can be gently removed. There are many kinds of grafts that "took," but that's not good enough. Peyote grafting must result in new growth in order to be successful. The best stocks should always be used for this sacrament. With tubercle grafts (chunk or slice) the chances of survival are slimmer but not improbable. The piece may not show growth for up to a month or more then suddenly start growing new heads.

Any arms the stocks begin to throw are removed immediately, as these divert energy away from the scion. These plants can be drenched; the chances of rotting are fairly slim. Every time the majority of pots are dry, they should be watered. Fertilizer may be used according to personal preference.

If grafting begins in March, by October there will be large specimen-size plants. If larger than normal stocks are used, the results could be huge, flowering, multi-headed, great-grandparent peyote plants in about one year. Most people prefer to cut these impressive plants off the graft stock and re-root them. To re-root the plants requires some patience. Experts don't recommend eating peyote buttons after they've been dipped in root hormone. Smart cultivators use agricultural sulfur or let the buttons throw roots on their own.

Experiments have shown that for re-rooting purposes, sizable side shoots respond better than the main top. These are sliced clean and kept inverted for a few days to callous properly. To stimulate root growth, the buttons are placed up-right on a wooden surface near the other peyote so that they can adopt the same watering schedule. The bottoms of the new buttons will dry out more rapidly than the others. This watering-drying routine coaxes the heads to send roots within weeks. These plants require very carefull treatment, because their fragile roots may break and, if so, will rot very easily. In about one and a half years a nice complete tap root will form, and the alkaloidal spectrum will undoubtedly balance out too.

Eventually the cultivator will have gotten so many seeds, seedlings, and pups that grafting will become an unnecessary step and seed grown medicine will become one's forté.

TROUBLESHOOTING PLANT PROBLEMS

 The greenhouse and cacti need to be be inspected regularly for pests and other problems. Thrips and mealy bugs are fairly common, especially on soft-skinned cacti. Thrips are extremely small and look like tiny white footballs. They tend to hide out in the trichomes (the wool) and feed off new growth causing it to scar. Mealy bugs generally attack the roots and can be detected on the bottoms of pots by cottony, white, web-like stuff along with scurrying, little insects resembling pill bugs. Mealy bugs are often found on a plant that is not responding to waterings while the others are obviously hardy.

Thrips can be eliminated by spraying with pyrethrenes, an organically derived pesticide. This is fairly safe for *Lophophora*, but will damage or destroy *Trichocereus* (which doesn't host thrips, but is a common graft stock for peyote) unless it is rinsed within one or two minutes. The treatment should be done in the morning or evening. After a minute or two, the cacti should be rinsed and the residue washed into the soil to try and disinfect it too. Only the skin of *Trichocereus* seems to be affected by pyrethrenes; they have not been observed to cause harm by being in the soil.

Mealy bugs can be a serious problem. Their presence can cause root rot, and this may be the only indication of their presence, which most people might not notice otherwise. To combat mealys, the roots are thoroughly rinsed clear of soil and bugs with a garden hose and fingers. All of the white stuff must be completely removed. Then the roots are allowed to dry out fully. The infested cactus is treated again with pyrethrenes and rinsed. After the roots have dried out, the plant is repotted in dry soil and after a week is slowly reintroduced to water. The original container is discarded or cleaned, and surrounding plants are checked for contamination.

Scale, spider mites, burrowing larvae and grasshoppers are a less common problem. The scale looks like tiny, white or gray shingles and can be treated by lightly scraping and dosing with pyrethrenes or dilute rubbing alcohol. Spider mites enable mold and rot to form by making tiny holes in the tissue which can subsequently become infected; they can be sprayed as well. The cactus bore is the larval form of an insect that commonly lays its eggs on a prickly pear cactus. The next plants on their menu are myrtillo and grafted Lophophora. The easiest way to detect them is to discover their waste products built up at the door of their nests. Within days these critters will completely tunnel through a graft and down into the stock. They grow quickly, making wider tunnels that start to rot. To treat an afflicted cactus, the bad sections and the worm are cored out. Then the crud inside is rinsed out, and the plant is placed in the sun to callous. All of the plants in the area should be checked for indications. Grasshoppers eat the flowers, fruit pods, and sometimes the cactus itself. These are removed or destroyed before they grow in numbers and size causing considerable damage.

The two most common forms of rot work in different ways but may have the same results: dead plants. Damaged roots and frozen or waterlogged plants will be prone to rot that is characterized by a halt in growth, dropping of flowers, and wrinkled discoloration of the skin. If the damaged section is not sliced completely clean from the plant, the rot will spread to the center and thoroughly turn the cactus into mush. Orange rot starts with the formation of rust colored dots near the center of the cactus surface and spreads outward in diameter as well as inwards throughout the plant. It may not seem to be spreading, then suddenly the plant will look pale and weak. Upon slicing a section for further examination, "tunnels" are often discovered within the plant. All of the orange rot must be removed or it will spread again. Plants with these conditions should be placed in a warm, dry, well lit place.

Another common problem is too much light, which will cause an obvious burn on the sides facing the south or west. This will make San Pedro yellow, tough, and even more unpleasant to eat fresh. When peyote gets sunburnt, it first turns red to yellow to white and sort of blisters. Then that portion dries and turns into a papery scab that actually protects the underlying tissue. If these plants are moved into a more screened area, their tissues will actually heal similarly to human skin. Eventually peyote will totally recover. All of the above conditions can be treated naturally using predator insects or concentrated botanicals.

[pp 44-66 from "Cultivating Peyote and Other Cactii" text and photos © 1997 by Derek Westlund, reprinted by permission.]

More about peyote, its sacramental use, and cultivation can be found in:

Peyotl: The Medicine Journal
2509 N. Campbell Ave., Suite 128
Tucson, AZ 85719

$20 per year (4 issues)
$5 sample issue

Send S.A.S.E. for informative flyer, availability and pricing of legal specimen cacti, false peyotes, and other grafted oddities (not for consumption). Also available are Arizona cannabis/controlled substance tax stamps (sold as a novelty item only). Make checks payable to Derek Westlund. Please inquire. We would like to hear from you.

Ⓘncreasing Ⓟotency

There are several factors which influence the production of mescaline and other related alkaloids in cacti. Presence of a wide variety of trace minerals is important. Occasional watering with Hoagland A-Z concentrate provides these minerals. 1 part concentrate is combined with 9 parts water, and the cacti are watered with this once every 2 months.

Experiments conducted by Rosenberg, McLaughlin, and Paul at the University of Michigan at Ann Arbor in 1966 demonstrated that dopamine is a precursor of mescaline in the peyote cactus. Tyramine and dopa were also found to be mescaline precursors but are not as immediate and efficient as dopamine. It appears that in the plant, tyrosine breaks down to become tyramine and dopa. These are recombined to form dopamine, which is converted to nor-mescaline and finally to mescaline. Some cultivators take advantage of this sequence by injecting each peyote plant with dopamine 4 weeks prior to harvesting. Much of the dopamine converts to mescaline during this time, resulting in a considerable increase of the alkaloid in the plant

A saturated solution of free base dopamine in a .05 N solution of hydrochloric acid is prepared and 1-2 cc is injected into the root of each plant; the same amount is injected into the green portion just above the root. The needle is inserted to the center of the plant; the solution is injected slowly; and the needle is allowed to remain in place for a few seconds after injection. It is best to deprive the plant of water 1-2 weeks before injection. This makes the plant tissues take up the injection fluids more readily. If dopamine is not available, a mixture of tyramine and dopa is used 6 weeks before harvesting for comparable results.

San Pedro and other mescaline-bearing cacti have been similarly treated for increased mescaline production. Injections are given at the base of the plant and again every 3-4 inches, following a spiral pattern up the length of the plant.

A series of booster injections can be given to any of these cacti every 6-8 weeks and once again 4 weeks before harvesting for greater mescaline accumulation.

There are reports of similar process to increase the macromerine and nor-macromerine content of Doñana cacti using tyramine or DL-norepinephrine as precursors. Injections should be given 20-25 days before harvesting. Series injections can be given 45 days apart for higher alkaloid accumulation.

Readers are cautioned that injection procedures such as those described above involving acids and controlled substances should be performed only in licensed labs by professional chemists.

Extracting Pure Mescaline

 The isolation of mescaline from cacti containing this alkaloid is not difficult to perform. The chemicals required for this process are readily available, but their purchase may arouse suspicion of government agencies. The equipment employed is not expensive or particularly complicated and can be constructed very easily from ordinary household items. The entire process can be carried out in any lab in a matter of hours. In the final stages one can verify the success of the procedure by actually watching the crystals of mescaline precipitate in the solution.

Readers are cautioned that extraction procedures involving acids, bases and volatile solvents are hazardous, potentialy explosive or toxic, and should only be performed by chemists in licensed labs.

A kilogram of the cactus is ground, placed in a large pressure cooker, covered with distilled water, and boiled for 30 minutes. The liquids are strained and saved. The pulp is returned to the pot, covered with water, and boiled again for 30 minutes. The liquids are strained and combined with the previous strained liquids. This process is repeated about 5 times or until the pulp no longer has a bitter taste.

Illustration A (Separation Funnel)

← Rubber Stopper
(remove when funneling)

← Mescaline & Benzene Solution

← Emulsion Layer
← Ring Clamp & Rack
← Water & H$_2$O Solubles

← Stop Cock

← Collection Jug

Illustration B (Jug and Siphon)

← Rubber Tubing
← 2-Hole Rubber Stopper

← Glass Tubing 1/4" above Emulsion

← Mescaline & Benzene Solution

← Emulsion

← Water & H$_2$O Solubles

Collection Jug

The pulp is discarded, and the volume of the combined strainings is reduced by boiling in an open pot. Aluminum ware should not be used. When the liquids have been concentrated to the thickness of cream (about 1 quart), the heat is turned off and 400 g of sodium hydroxide (lye) is stirred in. This makes the mescaline more soluble in benzene and less soluble in water.

If a large separatory funnel is available, the liquids are poured into it, and 1600 ml of benzene is added *(see Illustration A)*. The funnel is shaken well for 5 minutes and left to stand for 2 hours. If a separatory funnel is not available, the process can be carried out in a one-gallon jug with a siphon attached *(see Illustration B)*.

After standing for 2 hours, the water layer will settle to the bottom and the benzene layer will float to the top. Between the two layers will be a thin emulsion layer of mixed water and benzene. The water and emulsion layers are drained off, if a separatory funnel is used; or the benzene layer is siphoned off, if the makeshift jug-siphon apparatus is used.

Neither the water nor the emulsion layers are allowed to get into the benzene layer when separating. If any of these layers get into the benzene during separation, everything is poured back into the separator and left standing. The separation is then repeated more carefully. Is some benzene layeris left in the water and emulsion it is not of great consequence, but it is important not to get the water or emulsion in the benzene. Nothing is wasted. All of the benzene which contains the mescaline is eventually salvaged in repeated extractions.

Sometimes the layers will fail to separate properly. If this is the case, the funnel or jug is immersed in a deep pot of hot water for 2 hours. This will break up the emulsion and bring about the separation.

A solution of 2 parts sulfuric acid and 1 part water is prepared. *(CAUTION: Water must never be added to acid or it will splatter; the acid is added a little at a time to the water by pouring it down the inside of the graduate or measuring cup containing the water.)* 25 drops of the acid solution are added 1 drop at a time to the benzene extracts. The jug is stoppered, shaken well for 1 minute, and left standing for 5 minutes.

White streaks of mescaline sulfates should begin to appear in the benzene. If these do not appear, the jug is shaken more vigorously for 2 or 3 minutes and allowed to settle for another 5 minutes. When extracting mescaline from San Pedro, it is sometimes necessary to shake the mixture more thoroughly and for a longer time in order to get the mescaline streaks to form. This is probably because of the lower mescaline content of the plant. This would also apply to any peyote that does not have a high mescaline content.

After the streaks appear, 25 more drops of the acid solution are added in the same manner. The solution is shaken as before and allowed to settle for 10 minutes. More streaks will appear. 15 more drops of acid are added, and the solution is once again shaken and allowed to settle for 15 minutes. Finally, 10 drops are added, and the solution is shaken and allowed to settle for 30 minutes. The solution is tested with wide range pH paper. It should show that the solution is between pH 7.5 and 8. The mescaline sulfate crystals are allowed to completely precipitate. As much of the benzene as possible is siphoned off without disturbing the crystals on the bottom of the jug.

The next steps are for salvaging any mescaline still in the water and emulsion layer. The benzene siphonings are combined with the water/emulsion layer, shaken well for 5 minutes, and left to settle for 2 hours as before. The benzene layer is carefully removed and treated again with acid. The crystals are allowed to precipitate, and the benzene is siphoned off as in the previous steps. The siphoned benzene is recombined with the watery layer. This is repeated again and again until no more crystals precipitate. As much benzene as possible is siphoned off without drawing through the siphon.

The next step involves removing the remaining benzene from the crystals. There are two methods. The first is the quickest, but requires ether, which is dangerous and often difficult to procure *(see Illustration C)*. The crystals are shaken up with the remaining benzene, and the solution is poured into a funnel with filter paper. After the benzene has passed through the filter, the jug is rinsed with 100 ml of ether to salvage any crystals in the jug, and the ether is then poured over the crystals in the filter. After the ether has passed through the filter, the rinsing is repeated with another 100 ml of ether. The crystals are allowed to dry.

If ether is not available or if use of such a highly combustible substance is not desired, the second method can be used *(see Illustration D)*. The precipitate and

Illustration C

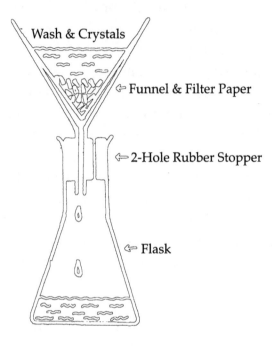

Wash & Crystals

⇐ Funnel & Filter Paper

⇐ 2-Hole Rubber Stopper

⇐ Flask

Illustration D

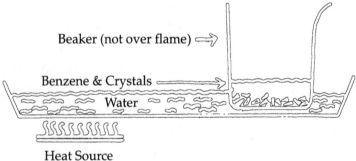

Beaker (not over flame) ⇒

Benzene & Crystals ⟶

Water

Heat Source
(electric or gas)

residual benzene is poured into a beaker. The jug is rinsed several times with a little benzene, and this is added to the beaker so that no crystals are left behind. The beaker is then placed in a heat bath until all of the benzene has been evaporated.

The next step is to purify the mescaline sulfate crystals. After either of these methods has been carried out, the dry crystals are dissolved in 200 ml of near-boiling distilled water. A pinch of activated charcoal (Norite™) is added, and the solution is filtered while still hot through #2 filter paper. The hot water which contains the mescaline will pass through the filter. The Norite absorbs impurities from the mescaline which may have impregnated the filter paper. A 10% ammonia solution is added a few drops at a time to the hot filtrates until the solution registers between pH 6.5 and 7. A boiling stone is placed in the solution and its volume is reduced to 75 ml by boiling. The boiling stone is removed, and the solution is allowed to cool to room temperature.

The solution is placed in a freezer or in a refrigerator turned up to the coldest possible temperature and allowed to cool almost to freezing. Tiny, white, needle-like crystals will form around the bottom and sides of the beaker. The crystals are broken up with a glass stirring rod while the solution is still ice cold. The solution is poured through a filter. Mescaline sulfate is insoluble in near freezing water and will not pass through the filter. The beaker is rinsed with fresh ice water, and then the water is poured over the filter. The crystals will now be pure white and can be dried under a heat lamp or in an oven at 250° F.

More mescaline can be salvaged from the water that has passed through the filter by boiling these liquids down to about 20 ml, adding Norite while hot, and filtering through #2 paper as before. The filtrate is chilled to near freezing once more, filtered while cold, and rinsed with ice water. The resulting crystals are allowed to dry. This repetition usually obtains at least 2 more grams of mescaline sulfate. If large volume mescaline extraction is being conducted, this salvaging procedure may be repeated several more times in order to maximize the extraction.

Jeremy Bigwood

Mescaline sulfate crystals

Mixed Alkaloid Extractions

 There are numerous methods for extracting a mixture of alkaloids from cacti. Different methods result in varying degrees of purity. For example, the dried, pulverized material can be defatted with petroleum ether prior to extraction to remove lipid content. Solvent combinations such as methanol/chloroform/ammonium hydroxide can be used for extracting. The extractions can be made less alkaline (pH 9.5) with 1-N hydrochloric acid, filtered, and washed in a separatory funnel (or improvised siphon-jug apparatus) with diethyl ether, neutralized with ammonium hydroxide, and evaporated to dryness.

Procedures involving solvents are difficult for non-professionals and may explode if handled improperly. In addition, some of the active principles may be non-alkaloidal. Too much purification might remove some of the active substances. The approach described here uses materials which may be purchased inexpensively and are somewhat safer to work with. This procedure extracts all of the alcohol- and water-soluble alkaloids and non-alkaloidal materials and permits only the fibrous pulp to be discarded.

Readers are cautioned that procedures involving volatile solvents may be hazardous, explosive or toxic, and should be performed in licensed labs.

The dried cactus is pulverized (tufts and spines need not be removed). A mixture is prepared from 2 parts isopropyl rubbing alcohol and 1 part clear, non-sudsing, unscented, and untinted ammonia water. The pulverized material is soaked in this mixture and allowed to stand covered overnight. Aluminum or iron-wares must not be used during any of these steps. After soaking, the mash is covered with isopropyl alcohol and boiled in a heat bath for 6 hours. The liquids are strained through muslin cloth, and as much liquid as possible is pressed from the pulp. The boiling and straining are repeated 3 more times with fresh alcohol. The strained liquids are combined.

The combined liquid is evaporated in a heat bath until only a tar remains. When evaporating a solvent, an electric range or hot plant (rather than a gas flame) should be used. There should be adequate ventilation, and one should avoid breathing the fumes. A fume hood with a spark-free electric fan is useful in this situation. The safest and most practical way to conduct a solvent extraction is to use an herbal extraction device.

The tar can be further dried by spreading it thinly on a baking tray and placing it in an oven set at the lowest possible heat. The tray is removed once every 15 minutes to examine the material. When it appears to be almost dry, it is placed back in the oven. The heat is turned off, and the tray is left there until the oven cools.

DICTIONARY OF CACTUS ALKALOIDS

Anhalidine: A tetrahydroisoquinoline alkaloid (2-methyl-6,7-dimethoxy-8-hydroxy-1,2,3,4,-tetrahydroisoquinoline) found in the *Lophophora* and *Pelecyphora* species.

B-O-methylsynephrine: A phenolic B-phenethylamine found in citrus leaves and some cacti. No data on its pharmacology, but a similar compound B-O-methylepinephrine produces considerable CNS stimulation.

3-dimethyltrichocereine: A B-phenethylamine alkaloid (N,N-dimethyl-3-hydroxy-4,5-dimethoxy-*b*-phenethylamine) found in the *Pelecyphora* species and some *Trichocereus* species.

Dolichotheline: An imidazole alkaloid properly known as N-isovalerylhistamine or 4(5)-[2-N-isovalerylaminoethyl] imidazole. It is found only in the *Dolichothele* and *Gymnocactus* species. Its pharmacological action is still unknown.

Homoveratrilamine: A dimethoxy form of the mescaline molecule (3,4-dimethoxy-*B*-phenethylamine). It has no activity by itself but may alter the mescaline experience slightly when taken in combination. It is found in San Pedro cactus and the urine of certain types of schizophrenics.

Hordenine: A phenolic *B*-phenethylamine found in barley roots and several cacti. It is also known as anhaline (N,N-dimethyltyramine) and has mild sympathomimetic activity and an antiseptic action.

Macromerine: A nonphenolic *B*-phenethylamine (N,N-dimethyl-3,4-dimethoxy-*B*-hydroxy-*B*-phenethylamine) found only in the *Coryphantha* species. It is reputed to possess 1/5 the potency of mescaline.

Mescaline: A nonphenolic *B*-phenethylamine (3,4,5-trimethoxy-*B*-phenethylamine). It is the main psychoactive component of peyote, San Pedro, and several other *Trichocereus* species and is also found in trace amounts in the *Pelecyphora* species.

Metanephrine: A weak sympathomimetic found in the *Coryphantha* species.

3-methoxytyramine: A phenolic *B*-phenethylamine discovered in the plant kingdom for the first time in San Pedro cacti. It is also found in the urine of persons with certain types of brain disorders and with cancer of the nervous system.

N-methyl-3,4-dimethoxy-B-phenethylamine: It is found in *Pelecyphora aselliformis, Coryphantha runyonii,* and the *Ariocarpus* species but not in peyote. It has some slight activity in the depletion of cardiac norepinephrine.

N-methylphenethylamine: A nonphenolic B-phenethylamine alkaloid recently found in the *Dolichothele* species. It is also found in the *Acacia* species and in other plants. Goats and sheep in Texas sometimes eat *Acacia berlandia* and suffer a condition known as limberleg or Guajillo wobbles. Pressor action of this alkaloid has been experimentally shown to occur with low toxicity. Phenalanine and methionine are its biosynthetic precursors.

N-methyltyramine: A phenolic B-phenethylamine found in some cacti, mutated barley roots, and a few other plants. It is probably an intermediate phytochemical step in the methylation of tyramine which occurs during the formation of candicine. It has a mild sympathomimetic action and probable antibacterial properties.

Normacromerine: A nonphenolic B-phenethylamine (N-dimethyl-3,4-dimethoxy-B-hydroxy-B-phenethylamine) found in the *Coryphantha* species. It shows a lesser effect on rats than does macromerine.

Pellotine: A tetrahydroisoquinoline alkaloid (1,2-dimethoxy-8-hydroxy-1,2,3,4-tetrahydroisoquinoline) found in the *Lophophora* and *Pelecyphora* species.

Synephrine: A phenolic B-phenethylamine (N-methyl-4-hydroxy-B-phenethylamine) found in citrus plants, some cacti, and human urine. It is a well known sympathomimetic agent and is probably an intermediary in the phytosynthesis of macromerine.

Tyramine: A phenolic B-phenethylamine found in several cacti. It is a mild sympathomimetic with some possible antiseptic activity.

SUPPLIERS

 The following companies sell some of the cacti (and their seeds) mentioned in this book. Before an order is placed, a catalog should be requested. It is usual to enclose $2.00 to cover the cost of the catalog and postage.

AZTEKAKTI
P.O. Box 26126
11306 Gateway East
El Paso, TX 79926

Basement Shaman
P.O. Box 1255
Elgin, IL 60121
Phone: (847) 695-2447
E-mail: bshaman@interaccess.com

Sells *T. pachanoi* (live specimens and unrooted and rooted cuttings), *Echinocereus triglochidiatus* (live specimens), and several species of *Mammillaria* (live specimens). In 1997 they will offer live specimens of *Trichocereus peruvianus*. They now accept credit card orders via phone. Send $2.00 for a catalog.

Cactus Unlimited
21030 Gardena Dr.
Cupertino, CA
Phone: (408) 257-1047

Send $3.00 for a catalog.

Desert Nursery
1301 S. Copper
Deming, NM 88030
Phone: (505) 546-6264

Horus Botanicals
HCR 82 Box 29
Salem, AR 72576

Sells *T. pachanoi* seeds. Send $3.00 for a catalog.

JLF
P.O. Box 184
Elizabethtown, IN 47232
Phone: (812) 379-2508

Offers dried San Pedro and various other exotic, and sometimes poisonous, botanicals for non-consumable purposes only.

Mesa Garden
P.O. Box 72
Belen, NM 87002
Phone: (505) 864-3131
Fax: (505) 864-3124
E-mail: cactus@swcp.com

This is a great source for a wide variety of specimens. They carry 30 varieties of *Trichocereus* species including *T. pachanoi* and *T. peruvianus*. Send 2 stamps for a catalog.

New Mexico Cactus Research
P.O. Box 787
Belen, NM   87002
Phone: (505) 864-4027

Good source for varying grades of very reasonably priced San Pedro and Doñana. Best selction of *Trichocereus* cuttings. Send $1.00 for a catalog.

... of the jungle
P.O. Box 1801
Sebastapol, CA 95473

Offers San Pedro cuttings and various *Trichocereus* seeds. Great source of other exotic botanicals. Send $2.00 for a catalog.

Timberwolf Gardens
P.O. Box 264
Fords, NJ 08863

Sells live San Pedro. Free price list with SASE.

Wildflowers of Heaven
P.O. Box 1989
Ranchos de Taos, NM 87557

A source for *Trichocereus pachanoi, T. peruvianus*, Doñana, and many other ethnobotanical seeds. They also offer cactus grafting and seed growing reports and cactus growing kits. Send $2.00 for a catalog.

TELR
Richard Glen Boire's Quarterly Legal Update on Shamanic Inebriants

Since time immemorial humans have used entheogenic substances as powerful tools for achieving spiritual insight and understanding. In the twentieth century, however, many of these most powerful of religious and epistemological tools were declared illegal in the United States and their users decreed criminals. The shaman has been outlawed. It is the purpose of *The Entheogen Law Reporter (TELR)* to provide the latest information and commentary on the interspace of entheogenic substances and the law.

TELR is a micro-circulation publication funded solely by subscription. Presently, no outside advertising is accepted. A one-year (4-issue) subscription for individuals remains $25 within the USA, and $35 internationally. Institutional subscriptions are $55 worldwide.

Subscriber information is strictly confidential and will be released only under court order. Your name will not be sold or given away.

Subscribe Me !

Name: _____ State: _____

Street: _____ Zip Code: _____

City: _____ E-Mail: _____

Mail cash, check or money order to:
spectral mindustries
POB 73401-PO, DAVIS/CA 95617-3401

T E L R

LAW ¡ POLICY ¡ COMMENTARY

AND

CONTROL THEORY

CONCERNING

SHAMANIC INEBRIANTS

Ronin Books for Independent Minds

SACRED MUSHROOMS & THE LAW .... Boire SACMUS 12.95 ___
Cognitive liberty, review of Federal & State laws & possible defenses.

THE HEALING MAGIC OF CANNABIS .... Potter/Joy HEAMAG 14.95 ___
Healing power of psychoactivity, tinctures, food, list of med conditions.

PSYCHEDELICS ENCYCLOPEDIA .... Stafford PSYENC 38.95 ___
LSD, peyote, marijuana and hashish, mushrooms, MDA, DMT, yage, iboga, etc.

MARIJUANA LAW, 2ND EDITION .... Boire MARLAW 17.95 ___
Increase privacy protections and reduce exposure to arrest.

CANNABIS ALCHEMY .... Gold CANALC 16.95 ___
Classic and modern techniques to enhance potency.

GROWING EXTRAORDINARY MJ .... Gottlieb GROEXT 12.95 ___
Sea of green, perpetual harvest techniques, nutrients, lights

LEGAL HIGHS .... Gottlieb LEGHIG 12.95 ___
An encyclopedia of relatively unknown legal psychoactive herbs & chemicals.

GROWING THE HALLUCINOGENS .... Grubber GROHAL 12.95 ___
How to cultivate and harvest legal psychoactive plants.

ACID TRIPS & CHEMISTRY .... Cloud ACITRI 16.95 ___
History, blotter, ergot rye, chemistry, bad trips.

MARIJUANA BOTANY ....Clarke MARBOT 24.95 ___
Sexing, cultivation, THC production and peak potency, continued production.

MARIJUANA CHEMISTRY .... Starks MARCHE 24.95 ___
Species, seeds, grafting, and cloning, growing techniques and essential oils.

CULTIVATOR'S HANDBOOK OF MARIJ ....Drake CULMAR 24.95 ___
Land and light concerns, harvesting and curing, psycoactive tobacco

LITTLE BOOK OF KETAMINE ....Kelly LBKETA 12.95 ___
"K" the psychedelic heroin, history, use, K-heads, dangers.

PASS THE TEST .... Potter/Orfali PASTES 16.95 ___
How tests work, how to beat test, what to do if tested positive.

GROWI NG WILD MUSHROOMS .... Harris GROWIL 12.95 ___
Step-by-step guide for growing wild & hallucinogenic mushrooms indoors.

PEYOTE & OTHER PSYCHOACTIVE CACTI .... Gottlieb PEYOTE 12.95 ___
Cultivation, grafting, cloning, nutrients, extractions, glossary of alkaloids, suppliers.

PSILOCYBIN PRODUCTION .... Gottlieb PSIPRO 12.95 ___
Species, spore prints, culture techniques, harvesting, extraction, suppliers.

Books prices: SUBTOTAL $_____

CALIF customers add sales tax 8.75% $_____

BASIC SHIPPING: (All orders) **$6.00**

Make sure to add in the per book shipping fee to Basic Ship fee - essential!

+ SHIPPING: add USA+$1/bk, Canada+$2/bk, Europe+$7/bk, Pacific+$10/bk $_____

Books + Tax + Basic + Shipping: TOTAL $_____

MC _ Visa _ Disc _ Exp date _ _ - _ _ card #: _

Phone # (Req for CC orders)_ _ _ _ _ _ _ _ _ _ _ _ _ _ _ Signature_ _ _ _ _ _ _ _ _ _ _ _ _ _ _ _ _

Name_ _

Address _ _ _ _ _ _ _ _ _ _ _ _ _ _ _ _ _ _ City _ _ _ _ _ _ _ _ _ _ _ _ _ State _ _ _ ZIP _ _ _ _ _

Make checks payable to **Ronin Publishing, Inc.**

POB 22900, Oakland, CA 94609 • Ph: 800/858-2665 • Fax: 510/420-3672

orders@roninpub.com • www.roninpub.com • Catalog online

Call for free catalog • Wholesale queries welcome • Prices subject to change w/o notice